"With tenderness and power, C. J.'s newest book illustrates the critical difference between snacking on the benefits of the cross and surveying the wonders of the cross. It's the difference between living as consumers and loving as the consumed...the difference between having a theology of grace and running boldly to the throne of grace. This is a must and magisterial read!"

SCOTTY SMITH, SENIOR PASTOR,
CHRIST COMMUNITY CHURCH, FRANKLIN, TENNESSEE

"My friend, C. J. Mahaney, has biblically shown Christians that Jesus Christ's role as our mediator is both gracious and joyous. What's more, he has theologically shown Him through this mediation to provide redemption and security. I will also pray that this book succeeds in evangelistically presenting to unbelievers the one mediator between God and men as Savior and Lord."

LANCE QUINN, PASTOR,
THE BIBLE CHURCH OF LITTLE ROCK

"*Christ Our Mediator* is a much-needed correction to this culture of entitlement. We've grown too accustomed to grace—we need to be floored by it. C. J. Mahaney gives us a fresh look at our Lord and His cross. I was drawn closer to Jesus through this book—what higher compliment could I offer?"

RANDY ALCORN, AUTHOR OF *THE GRACE AND TRUTH
PARADOX* AND *EDGE OF ETERNITY*

"The great nineteenth century Scottish pastor, Horatiu Bonar once wrote, 'If we would be holy, we must get to the cross and dwell there.' C. J. Mahaney takes us to the cross in such a way that we can indeed dwell there. This is a book to be read and reread many times. Its message will never grow old or out of date."

JERRY BRIDGES, AUTHOR OF *THE PURSUIT OF HOLINESS*

"C. J. Mahaney is one of our generation's most genuine and heartfelt proclaimers of the cross of Jesus Christ. In this unexaggerated book, readers will encounter the winsome zeal of a man who has found in Christ our mediator the greatest of treasures and a joy that must be shared."

DONALD S. WHITNEY, AUTHOR OF
SPIRITUAL DISCIPLINES FOR THE CHRISTIAN LIFE
AND *HOW CAN I BE SURE I'M A CHRISTIAN?*

LifeChange Books

CHRIST
OUR MEDIATOR

C. J. MAHANEY

Multnomah® Publishers *Sisters, Oregon*

CHRIST OUR MEDIATOR
published by Multnomah Publishers, Inc.

© 2004 by Sovereign Grace Ministries
International Standard Book Number: 1-59052-364-4

Cover design by David Carlson Design
Cover image by Keith Goldstein/Photonica

Unless otherwise indicated, Scripture quotations are from:
The Holy Bible, English Standard Version
© 2001 by Crossway Bibles, a division of Good News Publishers.
Used by permission. All rights reserved.
Other Scripture quotations are from:
The Holy Bible, New International Version (NIV)
© 1973, 1984 by International Bible Society,
used by permission of Zondervan Publishing House

Multnomah is a trademark of Multnomah Publishers, Inc.,
and is registered in the U.S. Patent and Trademark Office.
The colophon is a trademark of Multnomah Publishers, Inc.

Printed in the United States of America

For information:
MULTNOMAH PUBLISHERS, INC.
POST OFFICE BOX 1720
SISTERS, OREGON 97759

04 05 06 07 08 09 10—10 9 8 7 6 5 4 3 2 1 0

To Nicole, Kristin, Janelle, and Chad.
May our Lord give you as much joy
with your children as you have given me.

Contents

Acknowledgments

I want to thank my editor, Thomas Womack, for his invaluable contribution to this book. He has clarified and strengthened my attempts to communicate the glorious truth of *Christ Our Mediator*. This book wouldn't have been possible apart from the skillful help of this godly servant who through this project became a new friend.

And thanks to Joshua Harris, Kevin Meath, Jeff Purswell, Justin Taylor, Bob Kauflin, Brian Chesemore, and Steve Whitacre for your time, helpful editing recommendations, and meaningful encouragement.

Thanks to Nora Earles, who is simply the best secretary in the world.

Thanks to Covenant Life Church for your kind and consistent support in prayer as I wrote this book. For twenty-seven years you've been the dearest people on earth to me, and I'm the happiest pastor on earth because of you.

Most important, thanks to my extraordinary wife, Carolyn. There is no one I love or respect more than you.

SEARCHING
THE MYSTERY

Lest I forget Gethsemane,
Lest I forget Thine agony;
Lest I forget Thy love for me,
Lead me to Calvary
JENNIE EVELYN HUSSEY

The restaurant was uncrowded, and among the handful of early-evening diners were my wife and me on our date night. In the room's relative quietness, we could easily hear some of the conversation coming from the three parties seated not far away. At all three tables, the topic of extended discussion was Mel Gibson's film *The Passion of the Christ.* Hearing their talk, I felt a renewed sense of burden.

I'd first seen the movie myself only a few days earlier. Watching people enter the theater, many in a casual and fairly talkative mood with popcorn in hand, I sensed they were largely unprepared for what they were about to see. The mood of the audience changed quickly once the film began. I couldn't help noticing several people nearby in tears. And when it ended, there was mostly silence among the slowly dispersing crowd, with only a few hushed conversations. For a culture accustomed to thinking of the cross mostly as a piece of jewelry, seeing this movie was obviously a jolting experience.

Because of the vast numbers of non-Christians who watched *The Passion of the Christ* and witnessed its excruciatingly violent yet realistic images, countless evangelistic opportunities have opened up for our church and for Christians worldwide. For that, I'm profoundly grateful.

Images, however, cannot adequately convey the gospel's *content*. The gospel message isn't visual; it's truth. It is truth to be believed, not simply a collection of images to be viewed. Scripture is clear: Faith comes by hearing, and hearing through the word of Christ.[1] It's only the *preaching* of the gospel, not the depiction of it, that God promises to accompany with saving effect.

Paul reminded the Galatians, "It was before your eyes that Jesus Christ was publicly portrayed as crucified."[2] These Galatians were not present, of course, for the actual crucifixion of Christ; but it had been vividly and effectively portrayed to them *through Paul's preaching of the gospel.*

Although *The Passion of the Christ* brought millions to an unprecedented awareness of *how* Jesus died, it could not adequately convey *why* He died, and so the pronounced burden I felt was this: How could we as Christians explain to these moviegoers the true reasons behind Gethsemane and Calvary, as Paul did? It would mean that whenever scenes from *The Passion of the Christ* replayed in these people's minds, they could sufficiently grasp *who this is* and *why this is happening.* Otherwise I feared that without a clarifying theological explanation, the movie's impact for most people would be only superficial, vague, and fleeting.

> Do we adequately understand the deepest reasons behind the cross?

But do we ourselves adequately understand the deepest reasons behind the cross? If not, how can we take hold of those reasons—not only to be more compelled in sharing the good news of God's grace with others, but also to more fully experience the gospel's "unsearchable riches"[3] ourselves?

We Never Move On

My earlier book, *The Cross Centered Life,* reminds Christians that the gospel is the matter of first importance, the one overarching truth that should define our lives. That book stresses the profound urgency of focusing all we are and everything we do around the gospel of the cross of Christ. For not only does the good news of the cross come first chronologically in our Christian experience, but it *stays* foremost in critical importance for creating and sustaining our joy and our fruitfulness—a fact we too often overlook. The cross climaxes the story line of the Bible as well as the story line of our lives.

As one Bible commentator expressed it (in one of my favorite quotations), "We never move on from the cross, only into a more profound understanding of the cross."[4] That's why our attention must continually be drawn back to what John Stott calls "that great and most glorious of all subjects—the cross of Christ."

In *Christ Our Mediator,* I hope to lead us in the pathway of that more profound understanding. I'm attempting in this book to follow the counsel of my historical hero, Charles Spurgeon, who wrote, "Abide hard by the cross and search the mystery of His wounds."[5]

Behind Christ's wounds are mysteries, mysteries that are revealed in Scripture. In *Christ Our Mediator*, we'll look carefully and study closely the purpose of our Savior's sufferings, from His agonized prayer in the garden to His cry of forsakenness on the cross. We'll look with more depth and detail at *why* He suffered and what He uniquely accomplished by His suffering in relation to God and for the sinner.

Throughout this book we want to let the Holy Spirit bring us "hard by" the cross—as near it as possible—and to "abide" there, staying and dwelling in its shadow. We want to unhurriedly observe the cross from sacred Scripture, pondering and reflecting on this event as we probe the mystery of Christ's wounds. We want to let the biblical writers take our hands and lead us where no movie can go.

More Real than Ever Before

But maybe there's a nagging question in your mind: Why linger at the cross at all? If we as Christians already believe in what Jesus died for, if we've already received the gift of salvation He purchased for us with His precious blood, isn't it time to give our full attention to more "mature" matters of living out our faith?

In the church where I've served since 1977, our consistent pursuit has always been to keep the gospel central in everything we do. We never assume that there's already sufficient understanding, appreciation, and experience of Jesus Christ and Him crucified.

Recently I received a thank-you e-mail from a young woman who recalled her reaction when she first heard me identify the gospel as our church's lasting passion and priority. She told me, "I remember sitting there thinking…

'What does he mean? Yes, we are saved because Jesus died for our sins. But don't we then focus on other aspects of the Christian life?'"

Meanwhile, under our teaching she began recognizing "that there was a problem deeper than my outward expressions of sin (harsh words, complaining, etc.)… I was learning about the sin in my heart and the motives at the root.… I vividly remember driving down the road one day, and God opening my eyes to see that I'm a wretched sinner to the very core of my being. In that second I thought, *What am I to do?!*

He lived as if Jesus Christ died only yesterday.

"Instantly I was clearly aware that this is why Jesus Christ came and died on a cross—for me.… I laughed out loud, and said, 'My God, only You could show me what a wretched sinner I am and make it the greatest news I've ever heard!' The truth of Jesus' sacrifice became more real to me than ever before."

More real than ever before. Luther once said he felt as if Jesus Christ died only yesterday; through what we experience together in this book's pages, I hope you'll learn to live the same way. As we cultivate our understanding and appreciation for the cross, as we live the rest of our earthly days feeling increasingly as if Jesus' death happened only yesterday, we'll be more and more astonished and overwhelmed by God's grace.

Only then will we more deeply understand and experience God's grace in a way that consistently engages our passion.

More Amazing

I received another recent expression of thanks from a man who concluded his letter with these words: "I am amazed by the power of the gospel over and over, and have increased in my own love of the Savior. I can't believe that I have been saved from what I deserve."

Amazed by the power of the gospel, over and over—can you say those words about your own experience as well? Do you continue to find your salvation an incredible miracle as you recall the judgment you genuinely deserve?

If not…what can bring about a change? What is it that can make the gospel of God and His grace more deeply and consistently amazing to us? In our busy lives, how can we more often be gripped by gratitude and enflamed in passion for the Savior…and cast off lukewarmness and dullness in our spiritual experience?

For me, grace is never more amazing than when I'm looking intensely at the cross, and I believe the same will be true for every child of God. There's nothing more overpowering and captivating to the soul than to climb Calvary's mountain with childlike attentiveness and wonder, with all the distractions and wrong assumptions cleared away.

That's what we'll aim for in these pages. We'll trust our Shepherd to show us the unique path of righteousness He walked, and to give us a profound glimpse into the depths of anguish it brought Him. It was an anguish infinitely darker than any death-shadowed valley you or I will ever pass through, but by better understanding His suffering, we'll grow in a consistent joy and zeal that will equip us for whatever trials God brings our way in the process of our sanctification.

> We'll trust our Shepherd to give us a profound glimpse into the depths of His anguish.

Worthy of an Angel's Tongue

Before going on, I have to confess something personal: Although on most days I recognize how inept and inadequate I am in various areas, I'm never more acutely aware of my inadequacy than when I address the suffering of Christ and its meaning. I savor this privilege, yet when I teach and preach these things I consistently find myself physically weakened and emotionally overcome. So I acknowledge my dependence on God's strength in articulating this message, while also affirming my confidence in the One whose strength is made perfect in our weakness

Our God is good, He is gracious, He is kind, and He is eager to glorify His Son and edify His people. So I proceed, full of faith in Him…and confident that by the Holy Spirit's prompting, you'll join me in tears and in unspeakably joyful gratitude as we climb up Calvary together and gain a deeper understanding of what really happened there, and the staggering reasons behind it.

The subject of the cross, Spurgeon once said, "is worthy of an angel's tongue. And this also is true: It needs Christ himself completely to expound it."[6] In humble agreement with this prince of preachers on the infinite worth and wealth of this topic, I add as well the prayer it prompted from Spurgeon: that God would "by his own Spirit expound it to your heart."

Meanwhile, to help you more consciously depend on that work of the Spirit, I've included suggested words of prayer for you, here and throughout this book:

Lord, cause my reading of this
book to be more than a mental exercise.
Prepare my heart so that through the message
on these pages I can experience afresh Your active presence.
Impress into my soul whatever it takes to make Your grace
more deeply and consistently amazing to me.
Enflame me with passion…grip me with gratitude…

Notes

1. Romans 10:17
2. Galatians 3:1
3. Ephesians 3:8
4. David Prior, *Message of 1 Corinthians: Life in the Local Church* (Downers Grove, Illinois: InterVarsity Press, 1985), 51.
5. Charles H. Spurgeon, *Morning and Evening,* January 4, evening meditation.
6. Spurgeon, in his sermon "Wherefore Should I Weep?" (October 22, 1876, Metropolitan Tabernacle).

Chapter One

THE DIVINE ORDER

*Oh, the havoc that is wrought, and the tragedy, the misery,
and the wretchedness that are to be found in the world, simply
because people do not know how to handle their own feelings!*
D. MARTYN LLOYD-JONES

I grew up playing sports, and basketball in particular has always been a favorite. Though I turned fifty last year, I often remind my younger friends and playing partners that "I still have game." I keep insisting that my quickness and three-point shot are as prime as ever—though I see in their eyes they don't entirely buy my self-assessment.

There's one thing, however, that I have to admit is particularly different from my younger days: I'm much more conscious of the importance of warming up before a game. I know from long experience that my muscles work best when they're prepared—stretched and warm instead of cold and tight.

We often need a warm-up just as much for our spiritual and mental muscles, and I think that's especially true in this book. Before we push forward in the demanding spiritual exercise of more deeply experiencing Gethsemane and Calvary, we need to limber up our spiritual and mental faculties by exploring the whole matter of our *feelings*, and how they affect our view of reality and the way we live in response to reality. This is a critical conversation I need to have with you…and it can make all the difference in how much this book means to you.

If we want our hearts to be moved by the cross, if we want our emotions engaged, if we want to be truly amazed…we have to start by putting our feelings in their proper place. So we need to slow down for a moment and contemplate God's order for truth-based living and thinking, an order which we have a sinful tendency to disregard.

How Do You Feel?

Have you ever considered how thoroughly most of us live by our feelings today—how feelings-focused we are? In a typical day, how often do you make decisions and evaluate reality based primarily on your emotions at the moment?

Take the process of reading this book, for example. My guess is that you've already encountered statements here and there that made you think, "How do I *feel* about this?" Perhaps without even being consciously aware of this reaction, you were judging the merit of my words according to the subjective feelings you experienced while reflecting on them.

If so, you're not alone.

Our common tendency is to habitually begin with the internal, the subjective, the experiential, then use those feelings and impressions to determine what we'll accept as being objective fact. We let our feelings tell us what's true, instead of letting the truth transform our feelings.

> We let subjective impressions determine what we'll accept as objective fact.

For most of us, this isn't something we practice only while reading a book or hearing a sermon. It's the fundamental mindset with which we approach practically everything. It's how we *live,* and we even explain our daily choices by saying, "I feel good about this," or, "I had a bad feeling about it."

We're conditioned to this approach not only by our sin but also by our culture, which incessantly entices us to follow our "heart" and do whatever makes us feel good—

along with the flattering assurance that nonstop feeling good is something we absolutely deserve!

It would be fine to follow our feelings if we could always be sure they're faithful to reality. But they aren't; their perspective on reality typically has huge blind spots. As a result, our emotions are flighty, fickle, and far too easily dominated by any number of influences—spilled coffee at breakfast, a traffic stall when you're running late, a cutting comment from a coworker. Our feelings simply cannot be trusted.

Seldom Amazed

Even when it comes to our spiritual life, at any given moment we direct and locate our faith in our emotional state rather than in clearly objective truth. We tend to ask God for more "experience," then assure Him that if He'll give it, we'll acknowledge and believe His truth. And one of the tragic results is that we're seldom amazed by the reality of the cross and of the gracious disposition of God toward sinners that the cross reveals.

It happens frequently, for example, in our corporate worship. As people around us sing words expressing profound gratitude to Jesus for His death on our behalf, we may disqualify ourselves from truly entering into this adoration of our Savior because our "passion" this morning is absent.

It can happen also when we open our Bibles. Before us is a passage with words like *redemption, Savior, gospel, justified.* But for now those words evoke little response in us, and unthinkingly we pass them over to find something else that might light our fire. And if the enthusiasm doesn't come quickly...well, we may just forget the whole thing. After all, who wants to spend the mental energy it takes to think carefully and intensely about the Scriptures? Who has time to study? Who has time to meditate?

And this is how serious it gets: In our arrogance, we invest our feelings (or lack thereof) with final authority rather than recognize that our emotions are unstable and unreliable, often hopelessly controlled by selfish pride, and riddled with lies—lies that "feel" like the truth.

> In our arrogance, we invest our feelings with final authority.

I've watched people yield to such lies repeatedly. It's a frightening experience to sit with individuals who actually insist that what they feel is ultimately more authoritative to them than what's written clearly in Scripture. They even somehow assume God is sympathetic to this attitude. But He is not. He would, in fact, identify it as the height of prideful arrogance—and God is unalterably opposed to the proud.

Our First Question

That's the bad news. The good news: He gives grace to the humble.[1] Who are the humble? The humble are those whose first response to objective truth from God's Word is not to ask, "How do I feel?" but to say, "I'm not going to let my faith be determined and directed by the subjective and the experiential. Instead I confess openly before God that I will believe the objective truth of His Word, regardless of how I feel."

> When we focus on truth, reliable feelings follow, anchored in truth.

Bible teacher D. Martyn Lloyd-Jones[2] once issued this warning: "Avoid the mistake of concentrating overmuch upon your feelings. Above all, avoid the terrible error of making them central." Anyone making this mistake, he adds, is "doomed to be unhappy," because of the failure to follow "the order that God himself has ordained."

And what is that order? Lloyd-Jones reminds us that "what we have in the Bible is Truth; it is not an emotional stimulus…and it is as we apprehend and submit ourselves to the truth that the feelings follow." When we focus first on truth, lo and behold, feelings follow! And they'll be *reliable* feelings, because they're anchored in truth. That's the divine order.

Lloyd-Jones then proceeds to this profound application: "I must never ask myself in the first instance: What do I feel about this? The first question is, Do I believe it?"

Getting Things in Order

He's exactly right. It doesn't mean we *never* evaluate how we feel; that's just not where we're to start when we encounter truth. The starting place is determining what we truly believe. Otherwise, we end up actually shortchanging ourselves emotionally and experientially, since deep and profound feelings are the inevitable effect of Scripture rightly understood and believed, and of worship entered into properly.

As you read and meditate and think seriously about what's in your Bible, and believe and accept it, then ultimately *you will indeed experience it,* and *you will feel the effect of it.* There's heart-transforming truth in the Scriptures, but you won't encounter it by first trying to feel it.

Knowing and wholeheartedly believing the truth will always bring you eventually to a trustworthy experience of the truth. But if you trust your feelings first and foremost, if you exalt your feelings, if you invest your feelings with final authority—they'll deposit you on the emotional roller coaster which so often characterizes our lives.

Please don't misunderstand. I'm not advocating a complete ignoring of our feelings. Nor am I criticizing genuine spiritual experience, the kind of vibrant passion for God that Jonathan Edwards referred to as "religious affections." Quite the opposite! I am in fact a passionate advocate of genuine spiritual experience and religious affections—*it's just not where we're meant to begin.* Our feelings are an essential part of our right response to reality, but they should never in themselves be the determiner of reality.

Let me ask you: Where do you consistently direct your faith? What does it rest on? Is it your emotional state...or the objective realities that the Word of God and the Spirit of God have revealed? When you read or hear biblical truth proclaimed, what internal conversation takes place in your soul? Is your first reaction, *What do I feel about this?*

If so, do you plan to continue submitting everything ultimately to your feelings? Or will you instead trust in God's testimony, so that whenever you encounter biblical truth, your initial question will always be, *Do I believe it?* That's the only reliable way to transform your emotions...and to take them into a realm of love and adoration for the Lord that you've never before experienced.

Where It Matters Most

The divine order begins not with ourselves, but with God. And in this book we'll see how putting God and His objective truth first, and our feelings second, is never more applicable or valuable than when we draw near the cross, which is the hinge and center of human history. It presents an unfathomably stunning reality that we do well to return to again.

One Sunday morning, Charles Spurgeon was the guest preacher at a church in a country town in eastern England. Seated behind him was his grandfather, who was also a preacher. Spurgeon was speaking that day on Ephesians 2:8—"For by grace you have been saved through faith. And this is not your own doing; it is the gift of God."

As Spurgeon carefully explained this glorious gospel of grace, now and again he would hear the encouraging voice of his grandfather behind him, saying gently, "Good! *Good!*" At one point, he even heard this gentle prod from the old man's voice: "Tell them that again, Charles."

And of course, Spurgeon did indeed "tell them that again."[3]

Most likely you're not a stranger to the gospel of grace and the basic truths of the cross of Christ. This book, however, is an opportunity for us to follow the wise exhortation of Spurgeon's grandfather and to see and hear these wonderful things again, more clearly than ever, so God's grace astounds us as never before.

Thank You, Father, for directing my attention
upward and outward to objective truth,
and away from self-centeredness
and enslavement to subjectivity.

I turn away from self-focused arrogance and toward You—
to receive forgiveness for that arrogance.
I direct my faith toward You and Your Word,
for You alone are worthy.

As my faith is built up and strengthened,
transform my emotions so that I more truly love You
with all my heart and all my mind and
all my soul and all my strength.

Notes

1. James 4:6; 1 Peter 5:5
2. Quotations from D. Martyn Lloyd-Jones in this section are from an excellent chapter on "Feelings" in his book *Spiritual Depression: Its Causes and Its Cure* (Grand Rapids: Eerdmans, 1965).
3. Spurgeon recounted this story years later in a sermon entitled "All of Grace," given at London's Metropolitan Tabernacle.

Chapter Two

THE DIVINE
DILEMMA

Men are opposed to God in their sin,
and God is opposed to men in his holiness.
J. I. PACKER

It was a crowded morning in Starbucks. I was standing with
several customers who formed two parallel lines leading
toward the counter. As my turn came to step forward and
order coffee, the young man serving me smiled and said,
"Hey, how are you?"

For a number of years I've been giving a particular
response to that frequent question. I do it as a way of
preaching the gospel to myself every day; I've also found it
at times to be an effective opening for sharing the gospel

with others. I used the words again that morning in Starbucks.

"Better than I deserve," I answered.

Immediately the guy behind the counter began challenging my self-assessment. He was moved, I think, by compassion and a genuine concern that I was unreasonably deficient in my self-worth. When I didn't buy his assurances, he seemed irritated. Finally he challenged me, "Have you killed anybody?"

"No," I told him, "no, I haven't murdered anyone." But I went on to talk about how serious my sin was. In that brief moment, I was able to introduce him to the doctrine of human sinfulness.

Worse than Lepers

Partway through the conversation, I turned to my right. The lady in the next line was staring at me, with a look as if to say, "I'd recommend decaf." In fact, the entire place seemed to be listening to my explanation.

I concluded by simply telling the young man, as I approached the point of tears, "I'm a sinner. And I need a Savior." And I meant it.

The conversation was ever so brief. When that moment was over, people around me seemed to gradually divorce themselves from what they'd heard and to return to whatever had earlier occupied their minds and hearts—still sadly unaware, I suspect, of how much they also needed a Savior. And unaware of what an unfathomable miracle it is that God allows their hearts to keep on beating.

R. C. Sproul wrote that the most perplexing theological question is not why there's suffering in this world, but why God tolerates us in our sinfulness. Considering how our sin must appear in the pure sight of the righteous and holy God who created us, why are we even still here, alive and breathing? God's mercy is indeed an incredible mystery.

> Considering how our sin must appear in God's sight, why are we even still alive and breathing?

Luke tells us of the time while Jesus was "on the way to Jerusalem," and He encountered ten lepers. From a distance, they begged Him for mercy.[1] Knowing of their condition, we easily understand their desperate cry. Yet our own innate condition is far more serious than leprosy. In Starbucks I was surrounded that morning by lepers, fellow lepers like me who were born with a spiritual disease infinitely more subtle and sinister and abhorrent than any leprosy or cancer or virus ever known. Yet we rarely grasp the terrible threat facing each of us in our human condition, and so even less often experience astonishment over what God has done on our behalf to meet that threat.

The word *amazement* is related to the word *maze,* and its root meaning has to do with being perplexed and bewildered. But when you tell non-Christians, "God loves you," they are not surprised, they are not stunned, they are not perplexed. Regrettably, the same is true among most evangelicals, who simply assume this gracious disposition of God—and therefore presume upon it. And we'll continue to do this until we learn to see our condition more fully from God's perspective.

The divine order requires starting with God rather than ourselves, and to start with God means gaining an understanding of our situation in His eyes as it stood *before* Christ's death.

For God, that situation involved a dilemma.

God's Insolent Opponents

Paul conveys this dilemma in the opening chapters of his first letter to Timothy. God is "the King of ages, immortal, invisible, the only God," Paul says.[2] As King of ages, He's the absolute Sovereign One who transcends time. In His immortality, He's immune to decay, to destruction, and to death. And He's invisible—living in unapproachable light, so that sinful beings cannot see Him and live. Furthermore, He's the *only* God, with no rivals.

In utter contrast to this is the portrait of humanity Paul paints for Timothy: "lawless and disobedient...ungodly and sinners…unholy and profane…those who strike their fathers and mothers…murderers, the sexually immoral, men who practice homosexuality, enslavers, liars, perjurers, and whatever else is contrary to sound doctrine."[3]

That's the biblical perspective on mankind—and all of us fit somewhere in that description.

Paul puts himself there as well, confessing that he'd been "a blasphemer, persecutor, and insolent opponent" of God.[4] Paul even identifies himself as "the foremost" of sinners, the worst sinner, the chief of sinners.[5]

For God, the divine dilemma comes about because He isn't indifferent to any of this sinfulness on mankind's part. He is, in fact, righteously and furiously opposed to every bit of it. He cannot simply overlook or excuse it. In light of His holiness and justice, He has no alternative but to punish sin and punish the sinner. In our court systems, a judge who simply overlooked people's offenses and "just forgave" them would quickly be kicked off the bench. God is righteous, and must do what is right in punishing unrighteous sin.

> God cannot simply overlook or excuse sin.

And yet, as Paul informs us, God "desires all people to be saved and to come to the knowledge of the truth."[6]

God's desire is to save—but how can He rescue anyone?

He's righteously opposed to sin, yet sin lurks in every corner of every human heart. We're all "lawless and disobedient," as Paul says; we're all "ungodly and sinners"; each of us to some degree can give ourselves the same self-description Paul does: an "insolent opponent" of God.

What an impossible predicament! A holy God can respond only in furious wrath to sin; how much more so when the sin is persistent, intrinsic evil! How could He ever forgive, pardon, save, and be reconciled with those who are entrenched and enslaved in such blatant hostility toward Him?

How?

If Only

Tucked away in the book of Job is an agonizing glimpse of this dilemma from a human perspective—plus a hint of the solution God will provide.

In the midst of his suffering, the man Job is acutely aware of God's holiness, and he fears his afflictions may be an expression of God's judgment. In this awareness, Job at one point cries out, "How can a mortal be righteous before God?" After all, he knows that God "is not a man like me that I might answer him, that we might confront each other in court."[7]

Locked in hopelessness, Job somehow summons this desperate longing:

If only there were someone to arbitrate between us,
to lay his hand upon us both,
someone to remove God's rod from me,
so that his terror would frighten me no more.[8]

If only… If only there were someone to arbitrate between a suffering man and a holy God. Such an arbitrator, such a mediator, could indeed touch us both, lay his hand upon us both. Then somehow I could escape the terror of God's judgment. Job saw clearly the impassable gulf between humanity and God, yet somehow he could envision an intermediary to bridge that impossible distance.

> In true reality, you and I are ready to die, with absolutely no hope…except to cry out for a mediator.

Can you place yourself in Job's sandals? In the true reality of the divine dilemma, that's exactly where you and I are in our humanity—ready to die under the righteous wrath of a holy Lord, with absolutely no hope…except to cry out for a mediator.

Answer to the Cry

We're quite familiar today in business and legal arenas with the process of mediation. Typically, two parties are in conflict, each feeling wronged or in imminent danger of being wronged by the other, but they share together a willingness to seek a solution through a neutral third party. This neutral mediator or arbitrator oversees the process of negotiation between the two parties, hoping for a measure of reconciliation and agreement that satisfies the perceived offense to both parties.

That picture is almost totally unlike the kind of mediation needed between God and humanity.

Both situations, it's true, involve parties in opposition. But in the conflict between God and man, only one party has been offended. God has been profoundly and acutely aggrieved by the other party; He Himself is fully innocent, entirely without fault or blame.

The other party (all of humanity) is undeniably, categorically, and completely guilty—yet this guilty party *does not even care to be reconciled,* but is locked in active hostility to the other party. In contrast, God is fully committed to resolution with the violators.

As we see this impasse more clearly…as we begin, by the convicting work of God's Spirit, to see and feel the weight of our own personal offense against God…we easily identify with Job's longing for a mediator who could "lay his hand upon us both."

The incredibly good news for all of us is that Job's desperate cry has been answered. There *is* someone to arbitrate between God and humanity. There *is* someone to touch us both.

Thank You, Father,
for Your awesome and blazing holiness.
Thank You that it can never be compromised or ignored.

I recognize the weight of my offense against You.
I acknowledge before You the uncrossable chasm
between Your holiness and my own sinfulness,
and my heart echoes Job's cry for a Mediator.

Notes

1. Luke 17:11–13
2. 1 Timothy 1:17
3. 1 Timothy 1:9–10
4. 1 Timothy 1:13
5. 1 Timothy 1:15
6. 1 Timothy 2:4
7. Job 9:2, 32 (NIV)
8. Job 9:33–34 (NIV)

Chapter Three

THE DIVINE RESCUE

The debt was so great,
that while man alone owed it,
only God could pay it.
ANSELM

She was what psychologists call a "cutter"—and a friend of mine (who's a pastor) wrote me a letter in which he described an unforgettable counseling session with this troubled young woman.

It was her mother who had asked for the meeting, as my friend explained to me: "She related how her oldest daughter had been in the emergency room four times so far that year. Three times she had cut herself so deeply that stitches were required. Another time she had taken a bottle of pills, survived, and was detained in a psychiatric ward for teenagers. Now back at home, her daughter had cut herself again." The pastor agreed to meet with the daughter.

Problem-Solving Blood

The next day, the woman's daughter walked into his office. My friend's letter explains how the session developed:

> She wore an oversized turtleneck with sleeves that went down almost completely over her hands. After a time of gentle questions and listening, the conversation turned to "cutting." She said that when she was upset with herself, or upset over the offenses of other people, she cut herself. It seemed to relieve the tension. Cleaning up from the bloody wounds distracted her from the other problems.
>
> She pulled up her sleeve and showed me her arm, and I don't think I will ever forget the sight. That image stayed in my mind for days and was painful every time I recalled it.
>
> What could I do? All I really knew about biblical counseling was to pray for people and to tell them about the gospel. Very small errors in a person's understanding of the gospel seemed to result in very big problems in that person's life.

The pastor pulled out a pad of paper and drew out for the young woman a diagram of the gospel. He agreed with her that blood can indeed "solve problems"—but pointed out that the blood "did not have to be her own, and that the cutting had already been done on her behalf. The Spirit brought illumination, and she prayed to accept the gospel."

> He pointed out that the blood did not have to be her own.

At the time the pastor wrote this to me, six months had passed since that meeting, and the young woman had gone the entire duration without cutting herself again.

Yes, it requires blood to solve our very worst possible problem. For God, who in His righteous wisdom determined that sin's just penalty is death, also determined that without the shedding of blood, there is no remission of sins.[1]

Our Mediator's work would be a labor of blood.

Key to the Bible

If you were searching for a single sentence in Scripture to best capture the story line and theme of the entire Bible, what would you choose? Where would you look?

Many of us would no doubt go right to the beloved and familiar words of John 3:16, with good reason. But let me suggest we search no further than the place in Scripture we've already visited, the opening pages of Paul's first letter to Timothy.

Fix your thoughts on this sentence:

> For there is one God, and there is one mediator between God and men, the man Christ Jesus, who gave himself as a ransom for all, which is the testimony given at the proper time.[2]

J. I. Packer says it isn't too much to describe these verses as "the key, not merely to the New Testament, but to the whole Bible, for they crystallize into a phrase the sum and substance of its message."[3]

In this one sentence, Paul succinctly captures the main theme and essence of the entirety of holy Scripture—as well as answering the desperate cry we heard from Job for someone to arbitrate between God and man. Yes, Paul declares, there *is* a mediator! There is someone to arbitrate between us, to lay His hand on us both and remove the rod of God's wrath so His terror frightens us no more. There's a unique intermediary between God and humanity: the man Christ Jesus, who gave Himself as the ransom for all. The Bible's complete message hinges on this one point.

Because of God's amazingly gracious heart toward those who thoroughly deserve only His wrath, He both planned for and provided this mediator to resolve the divine dilemma—a mediator who, through His blood, would accomplish a unique assignment utterly unlike any other work of mediation. In the mystery of His mercy, God—the innocent, offended party—offers up to death His own Son, to satisfy His righteous wrath and save the guilty party from it.

"The glory of the gospel," says R. C. Sproul, "is this: The one from whom we need to be saved is the one who has saved us."[4] John Stott expressed it this way: "Divine love triumphed over divine wrath by divine self-sacrifice."[5]

Unique Man, Unique Work

But how could Jesus accomplish such an extraordinary work of mediation? An intermediary needs to represent both sides equally, yet in the conflict between God and humanity, the two sides are by nature as far apart as possible. How can Jesus represent both in bringing them together?

> How could Jesus represent both sides equally?

Only someone both fully divine and truly human can effectively mediate between God and men, and Jesus is exactly that. He is unique—totally unlike anyone else. That's why Paul insists there is only "one mediator," just as surely as there is only "one God."

The work of mediation Jesus accomplished is likewise unique. Notice in Paul's statement how he transitions immediately from the Savior's birth—"the man Christ Jesus"—to His saving death—"who gave Himself as a ransom for all." Christ's death was the purpose of His birth; Calvary was the reason for Bethlehem. God sent His Son to live a uniquely perfect life and die a unique death as the substitute for our sins.

Both Like Us and Unlike Us

Since sin has been committed by man, therefore sin must be atoned for by a man. Only a human being can be the perfect substitute for other human beings. The debt and obligation and responsibility is mankind's alone. Neither you nor I, however, can atone for our sin to satisfy God's righteous requirements; our own disobedience already condemns us before a righteous God. Furthermore, we're captive to sin; it's humanly impossible for us to release ourselves from its grip. Even if somehow, from this moment forward, we steeled ourselves to stop sinning (which is impossible), our record is still stained by the sins of our past.

That's our condition—having no possible way to atone for our sin, nor any possible way to free ourselves from enslavement to it.

A divine rescue is necessary. We need a savior! And in order to be our savior, in order to pay our debt, this individual must be *like us* —not just God in a form that merely appears to be human, but someone fully and truly human. Yet he must be *unlike us* as well, because he must be sinless, since only a perfect sacrifice is acceptable. He must be fully God, and not simply a man with a limited set of divine powers and abilities.

Author Ron Rhodes gives us helpful insight on this:

> If Christ the redeemer had been only God he could not have died, since God by his very nature cannot die. It was only as a man that Christ could represent humanity and die as a man.
>
> As God, however, Christ's death had infinite value sufficient to supply redemption for the sins of all mankind. Clearly then Christ had to be both God and man to secure man's salvation.[6]

No one else could do it. *Only Jesus Christ,* truly God and fully man, could be our substitute and make this sacrifice. Only Jesus could ever stand in this unique place and position. This One who lived the only perfect life also died a completely unique death as a ransom for our sin. He paid the price you and I owed to the innocent offended party, God our Creator and Judge.

Only Jesus
Christ could do
it. No one
else could.

Therefore the offended party is appeased. His righteous wrath against our sin is satisfied, having been poured out not upon us, but on Christ.

God's holy hostility against us has ended. The divine dilemma is resolved.

That's what Christ's death means to God.

No Better News

And what does Christ's death mean for us—for all who turn from their sins and trust in this unique mediator?

First, we have peace with God—the actual, objective reality of peace with Him, because His holy hostility against us has been spent against Christ instead.

Second, we no longer face condemnation from God when our life on this earth is over. Every believer in Christ can know that the moment we pass from this world and stand before God the righteous Judge, the verdict to be announced in our case will be "not guilty," by reason of the righteousness of Christ.

With full assurance we can anticipate and even experience that verdict *right now*. Our lives here and now are transformed as we live today in the joyful light of *that* day. We live today free from the fear of wrath on that future date.

What amazing grace! There simply isn't greater news we could give to anyone, anywhere, at any time.

And you and I indeed have the privilege as well as the responsibility of proclaiming it. We've been entrusted with this unique message about this unique Mediator, and we're the sole guardians of it. That's why we must deeply understand it ourselves and take it to heart, so we can share it accurately and passionately with others.

And now—having brought these incredible realities of Christ's mediation into clearer focus—we can proceed to Gethsemane and ultimately draw near the cross to more deeply understand our Savior's suffering—and to become more affected by it.

Lord God, I exalt You as My Redeemer and Rescuer!

Father, thank You for the Mediator
whom You both planned for and provided
in Your love and mercy and wisdom and power.

Jesus, You alone could be my substitute
and pay the penalty for my sin!
How can I ever find adequate words to thank
You enough for Your uniquely perfect life
and Your uniquely perfect death on my behalf?
With all my heart and soul and mind and strength,
I thank and praise You for Your sacrifice.

Thank You for this truth that so transcends my emotions.
Continue to allow it to transform my emotions.

Notes

1. Hebrews 9:22
2. 1 Timothy 2:5–6
3. J. I. Packer, *God's Words: Studies of Key Bible Themes* (Grand Rapids: Baker, 1998), 109.
4. R. C. Sproul, *Saved from What?* (Wheaton, Illinois: Crossway Books, 2002).
5. John R. W. Stott, *The Cross of Christ* (Downers Grove, Illinois: InterVarsity Press, 1986), 15.
6. Ron Rhodes, *Christ Before the Manger* (Eugene, Oregon: Wipf & Stock Publishers, 2002), 205.

Chapter Four

STARING INTO
THE CUP

*The garden of Gethsemane is one of the most
sacred and solemn scenes in the entire Bible.*
SINCLAIR FERGUSON

It's a moment when our world stops turning. A change so abrupt, so pronounced, that it shocks our very soul.

Here's why it slams us so fast and hard: While we look at Jesus in the pages of the unfolding Gospels—allowing ourselves to walk closely alongside Him through those three exciting years of ministry—words like *authoritative, assured,* and *fearless* truly describe Him. He's unfailingly steady and controlled.

But there comes a moment, as we follow Him into "a

place called Gethsemane,"[1] when all is radically changed. Suddenly we encounter a Savior we're unfamiliar with. What we observe is foreign and frightening.

Jesus "began to be greatly distressed and troubled," Mark's Gospel tells us.[2] "He began to be gripped by a shuddering terror and to be in anguish," one translation renders it. Other versions use the words *horror, deep alarm, dismay.*

This is a consuming, crushing agony for Him, utterly unlike anything we've previously observed.

Nearly Dying

Remember those days in Galilee? We saw His extended hand offering one tender touch after another as He healed sickness and forgave sin. We saw His strong arms outstretched with power as He cast out demons and raised the dead. We saw Him striding serenely on the surface of a wave-tossed sea on a stormy night. We saw Him seated tranquilly in a little fishing boat in shallow, sun-sparkled water beside a shoreline packed with listening crowds astounded and delighted by His incomparable teaching.

On a grassy hillside, we saw genuine gratitude on His upraised face as He gazed into the heavens and blessed a few loaves and fishes; we caught His smile of compassion as He handed out the fragments to feed thousands. In awe we watched Him on a rocky, cloud-wrapped summit as His face and form were wondrously transfigured in supernatural light.

Then here in Jerusalem, in the crowded temple courts, our eyes were wide in amazement as He stood up to the religious establishment and confronted their hypocrisy without the slightest qualm of intimidation, even to the point of fashioning a whip and chasing out their moneychangers.

Consistently He has been bold, He has been brave, He has been calm.

It's true we've also seen Him tearful and disquieted; when He came to Bethany after His friend Lazarus died, He loudly groaned, and at the tomb He openly wept. But that was far different from the sheer torment we see overtaking Him now, under these twisting, moonlit branches of Gethsemane's olive grove.

Jesus turns to Peter and James and John and tells them, "My soul is very sorrowful, even to death." *Even to death!* This is no hype; He means it. The sorrow in our Savior's soul at this moment is so powerful and pronounced that He actually draws near to dying in His human experience—even now, several hours before the coming torture of the cross.

After urging these three disciples to be watchful, Jesus steps a short distance beyond…and staggers to the stony

> The sorrow in this moment is so pronounced, He actually draws near to dying.

ground.[3] So horrific is the burden upon Him that He cannot even remain in an upright position.

Unprepared

We are seeing Jesus more vulnerable and more human than we've ever known. And we can't escape one question:

Why?

Why this shuddering terror, this staggering distress?

Even this very night there was no prior indication of such anguish. Earlier this evening, with solemn dignity, He inaugurated the Lord's Supper with His disciples and led them in singing a hymn. It's true that in the upper room He "was troubled in his spirit"[4] as He foretold His betrayal, and that He informed the disciples they would "all fall away"—yet in almost the same breath He confidently reminded them, "But after I have risen, I will go ahead of you into Galilee."[5]

It's not as if Jesus is surprised by death's approach. He long ago determined to bear God's judgment for sin as our substitute, and for months He has discussed His death repeatedly with His disciples.

Nor is He avoiding or postponing the hour of sacrifice for which He came to this earth. Quite the opposite. When it was no secret to anyone that Jerusalem was a hotbed of hostility against Him, He was out in front of His disciples, leading them here without a trace of reluctance—so that "they were amazed, and those who followed were afraid."[6]

The fear and anxiety belonged to His followers, not to Jesus.

So nothing has prepared us for Gethsemane, for this abrupt horror, this deep distress.

And we wonder: Why now? *Why now?*

What It Meant to Him

Here's why: In this garden, our Savior is beginning to confront as never before the ultimate and deepest agony of Calvary—an agony that will go infinitely beyond any *physical* aspects of His suffering, as we'll see in this book.

For Jesus, the way to the cross will bring incomparable and unprecedented suffering of wrath and abandonment. His downward journey into those unspeakable depths begins to tumble steeply in this garden called Gethsemane.

And as we follow into the garden to observe Him, we have to remember we're in the deep end of the pool theologically. What transpires here is so far beyond our depth, and I find a verse from an old hymn particularly relevant:

> Oh help me understand it,
> help me to take it in —
> what it meant to Thee, the Holy One,
> to bear away my sin.[7]

We need divine assistance to "take it in," to absorb deeply what bearing away our sin meant to Jesus, the Holy One. That's what we're after—what it meant *to Him.*

The Detestable Drink

Step closer with me under the shadow of the trees…let's watch and listen.

As Jesus lies prostrate on the ground, we overhear Him praying: "Abba, Father, all things are possible for you. Remove this cup from me. Yet not what I will, but what you will."[8]

He's making this plea repeatedly. With His face to the ground, we can see sweat on His temples. He lifts His head, and His expression reveals an agony so intense that His sweat is "like great drops of blood falling down to the ground."[9]

His words tell us why: "Remove this *cup,*" Jesus pleads again. In this moment, there's no doubt what is dominating His heart and mind.

What is this cup? It is clearly a reference to the wrath of God for your sins and mine.

If we knew the Scriptures as Jesus does—Scriptures that no doubt have been much on His mind in these hours—we couldn't escape this reference. Isaiah 51:17 shows us this cup in God's extended hand—it's "the cup of his wrath," and for those who drink from it, it's "the cup of staggering." This cup contains the full vehemence and fierceness of God's holy wrath poured out against all sin, and we discover in Scripture that it's intended for all of sinful humanity to drink. It's your cup…and mine.

In the vivid imagery of the Old Testament, this cup is filled with "fire and sulfur and a scorching wind"[10] like some volcanic firestorm, like all the fury of the Mount St. Helens eruption concentrated within a coffee mug. No wonder Scripture says that tasting from this cup causes the drinker to "stagger and be crazed."[11] No wonder that when Jesus stares into this detestable vessel, He stumbles to the ground.

That's why there's shuddering terror and deep distress for Him at this moment. In the crucible of human weakness He's brought face to face with the abhorrent reality of bearing our iniquity and becoming the object of God's full and furious wrath.

Hell, Not Heaven

What Jesus recoils from here is not an anticipation of the physical pain associated with crucifixion. Rather it's a pain infinitely greater—the agony of being abandoned by His Father.

As one Bible commentator notes, Jesus entered the garden "to be with the Father for an interlude before his betrayal, but found Hell rather than Heaven open before him."[12] Knowing the hour for His death is fast approaching, Jesus has come here in need as never before of His Father's comfort and

> Opening before Him, Jesus found hell rather than heaven.

strength. Instead, hell—utter separation from God—is thrust in His face.

We hear Him cry out: Father—is there an alternative? Is there any way to avoid this? If there's a way this could pass from me, would you please provide that alternative?

Silence. We can see it in His face—Jesus receives no answer to this desperate entreaty.

A second time, then again a third, He pleads for an alternative to that horror of abandonment by His Father. *If* such an alternative existed, the Father would most surely provide it. But the obedient Son's plea to His loving Father is met with silence. *Why?*

Listen to this verse for the very first time: *For God so loved the world...* that He's silent at this moment when His Son appeals for an alternative.

This is what bearing our sin means to *Him*—utter distress of soul as He confronts total abandonment and absolute wrath from His Father on the cross, a distress and an abandonment and a rejection we cannot begin to grasp.

In this, our Savior's darkest hour...do you recognize His love for you?

Another Cup

Listen again to the precious and powerful words we hear Him repeat to His Father:

"Yet not what I will, but what You will."

"Yet not what I will, but what You will."

"Yet not what I will, but what You will."

Jesus is saying, "Father, I willingly drink this cup by Your command—I'll drink it all."

And He will. He'll drink all of it, leaving not a drop.

Not only will He leave nothing in that cup of wrath for us to drink…but today you and I find ourselves with another cup in our hands. It's the cup of salvation. From this precious new cup we find ourselves drinking and drinking—drinking consistently, drinking endlessly, drinking eternally…for the cup of salvation is always full and overflowing.

> He'll leave nothing in that cup for us to drink.

We can drink from this cup only because Jesus spoke those words about the other cup: "Yet not what I will, but what you will."

I will drink it all.

As we watch Jesus pray in agony in Gethsemane, He has every right to turn His tearful eyes toward you and me and shout, "This is *your* cup. *You're* responsible for this. It's *your* sin! *You* drink it." This cup should rightfully be thrust into my hand and yours.

Instead, Jesus freely takes it Himself…so that from the cross He can look down at you and me, whisper our names, and say, "I drain this cup for you—for you who have lived in defiance of Me, who have hated Me, who have opposed Me. I drink it all…for *you*."

This is what our sin makes necessary. This is what is required by your pride and my pride, by your selfishness and my selfishness, by your disobedience and my disobedience. Behold Him…behold His suffering…and recognize His love.

Jesus my Savior, thank You for saying
to Your Father in Gethsemane,
"Not My will, but Your will be done."

Thank You that when there was no other alternative—
even after You so desperately pleaded for one—
You rose from Gethsemane's ground and stepped forward
to the cross in obedience to Your heavenly Father,
even unto death. For if You had not done this,
I would have been lost forever to sin and death and hell.
Instead, because You drank the cup of God's wrath,
I can drink forever from the cup of salvation.
O Jesus, how can I thank You enough?

Notes

1. Mark 14:32
2. Mark 14:33
3. Mark 14:34–35
4. John 13:21
5. Mark 14:27–28 (NIV)
6. Mark 10:32
7. Katherine A. M. Kelly, "Give Me a Sight, O Savior."
8. Mark 14:36
9. Luke 22:44
10. Psalm 11:6
11. Jeremiah 25:16
12. William Lane, *Commentary on the Gospel of Mark* (Grand Rapids: Eerdmans, 1974), 516.

Chapter Five

YOUR FACE IN THE CROWD

We may try to wash our hands of responsibility like Pilate,
but our attempt will be futile, as futile as his.
For there is blood on our hands.
JOHN R. W. STOTT

We saw Jesus enter Gethsemane shuddering, His soul deeply distressed.

But when He emerges from the garden, He is no longer trembling and troubled. Instead we see Him composed and authoritative as He tells the disciples, "Are you still sleeping and taking your rest? It is enough; the hour has come. The Son of Man is betrayed into the hands of sinners. Rise, let us be going; see, my betrayer is at hand."[1]

What explains this transformation? Only His obedience.

Strength to Endure

Though there was silence in answer to the Son's request for an alternative to the cross, the Father hasn't withheld comfort and strength to His obedient Son. In fact, at the close of Christ's prayer in Gethsemane, "there appeared to him an angel from heaven, strengthening him."[2] That provision of strength will continue to sustain Jesus in the hours of trial and torture that quickly unfold.

An armed force, led here by Judas, comes to arrest Jesus, and we follow as they take Him away. His disciples flee into the night.

Why does Jesus have no reply to these bogus charges?

A few hours later we see the continued inner strength of Jesus as He stands before Pilate. He stays amazingly silent in the face of accusations from the chief priests and elders, so that Pilate asks, "Do you not hear how many things they testify against you?" Still Jesus gives no answer, so that the governor is "greatly amazed."[3]

Have you ever wondered, as I have, why Jesus has no reply to these bogus charges? It seems that He could easily persuade Pilate, who shows respect for Jesus, and who certainly has no affection for the chief priests and elders; he knows what they're about.

But Jesus knows this is the hour for which He was born. This is the reason He had come into the world, and He in no way wants to resist it. He was born to die as our mediator. You and I know we're going to die; what we don't know is when or how. But Jesus knew when, He knew how…and most importantly, He knew why.

As John Stott says, what dominated Jesus' mind was not so much the living of His life but the *giving* of it. This indeed was the Savior's own testimony: "The Son of Man came…to give his life as a ransom for many."[4] So He offers His accusers no rebuttal or protest, and Pilate is astounded.

Irresistible Force

The governor then tries to help Jesus by taking advantage of a Passover custom in which authorities free one prisoner whom the public most wants to see released. Pilate offers the gathered crowd a choice between Jesus and a "notorious prisoner"—a terrorist named Barabbas.[5]

Meanwhile Pilate, seated on the judgment seat, receives an extraordinary message from his wife. We look over his shoulder as he reads it. Her note mentions that she "suffered much" in a dream about Jesus; therefore she counsels her husband, "Have nothing to do with that righteous man."[6] Here is conspicuous support for the innocence of

Jesus—and further incentive for Pilate to let Him go.

While the governor reflects on his wife's appeal, we make our way to the gathered crowd and see the chief priests and the elders circulating skittishly among the people. They're urging everyone "to ask for Barabbas and destroy Jesus."[7]

Pilate puts away his wife's note. He stands and asks the throng, "Which of the two do you want me to release for you?"

All around us, the mob is fully incited. They quickly cry, "Barabbas."

"Then what shall I do with Jesus who is called Christ?"

The response—from "all" of them, Matthew tells us—is this: "Let him be crucified!"

"Why, what evil has he done?" the governor asks.

Everywhere around us, the mob shouts all the more: "Let him be crucified!"[8]

Luke emphasizes that the throng was "urgent," "demanding," and "loud," and that "their voices prevailed."[9] Here's a force that Pilate can neither suppress nor ignore.

There That Day

Let me ask you: With whom do you most identify in the events of this dark day? Of the many onlookers and participants in these scenes, whose actions are most like your own, if somehow you were also there?

For some it might be Peter, weeping bitterly in the predawn hours as the weight of his denial of the Lord bore down upon him.

For others it might in some way be the passerby Simon of Cyrene, who was forced to carry Jesus' cross for Him. Others would identify with the women who were followers of Jesus and who "stood at a distance watching these things."

In the events of this dark day, with whom do you most identify?

Some would perhaps choose Mary His mother, who was "standing by the cross of Jesus," enduring such unimaginable pain. Or the disciple John, who also was "standing nearby" and whom Jesus spoke to from the cross. Or the penitent thief, who from his own cross cried out to the Savior in faith, "Jesus, remember me when you come into your kingdom." Or the centurion who, after watching how Jesus died, was moved to say, "Truly this man was the Son of God!"

But let me tell you who I identify with.

I identify most with the angry mob screaming, *"Crucify Him!"*

That's who we should all identify with. Because apart from God's grace, this is where we would all be standing, and we're only flattering ourselves to think otherwise.

Unless you see yourself standing there with the shrieking crowd, full of hostility and hatred for the holy and innocent Lamb of God, you don't really understand the nature and depth of your sin or the necessity of the cross.

From Our Hand

As those shouts and screams from the mob grow in volume, what is it like for our Lord to look out upon these people? Even if you can't recognize yourself among the angry faces, or distinguish your own strident voice… *He* can. And in response to those sinful shouts and curses from you and me, Jesus yields to the sentence of death.

A great hymn from the pen of the Scottish pastor Horatius Bonar helps us realize our responsibility in the Savior's death sentence. It includes these lines:

> 'Twas I that shed that sacred Blood,
> I nailed him to the Tree,
> I crucified the Christ of God,
> I joined the mockery.

In making this point, my ultimate purpose is not to convict you of sin, but to convince you of grace. Unless you're deeply aware of your sin, and of what an affront it is to God's holiness, and of how impossible it is for Him to respond to this sin with anything other than furious wrath—you'll never appreciate grace, and it will never be amazing to you. Only those who are truly aware of their sin can truly cherish grace.

Because of me, Lord Jesus, You suffered.
I acknowledge freely that it's because of my sin
that You were humiliated and beaten
and led away to death, just as much as if I myself
had been there to mock and strike and scourge You.

What a gift of grace, that You would endure this
out of love of Your Father and love of me!

Notes

1. Mark 14:41–42
2. Luke 22:43
3. Matthew 27:12–14
4. Mark 10:45
5. Matthew 27:15–17
6. Matthew 27:19
7. Matthew 27:20
8. Matthew 27:21–23
9. Luke 23:23

Chapter Six

THE SCREAM OF THE DAMNED

*This cry represents the most agonizing
protest ever uttered on this planet.
It burst forth in a moment of unparalleled pain.
It is the scream of the damned—for us.*
R. C. SPROUL

As the terrible events of this day continue to unfold, our sinful humanity is shown at its worst. The soldiers spit on him and strike him on the head. They strip Jesus, drape a scarlet robe on His shoulders, push a crown of twisted thorns on His head, and place a reed in His right hand. Kneeling before Him, they mock Him: "Hail, King of the Jews!"[1]

Ironically, their mocking words are in fact revealing truth. Their victim is not only King of the Jews, but God's appointed King over all creation, and one day every knee will bow before Him, including those of these soldiers who torture Him.

Prophetic Mockery

You and I follow along as the Romans lead Jesus away to the hill called Golgotha—"Place of a Skull." They nail His quivering flesh onto a cross, then raise it and slam it into the ground.

Luther said that we all carry in our pocket His very nails. Are you aware of those nails in your possession?

It isn't the nails that kept Him on the cross.

From all around us in the throng of onlookers, the verbal abuse continues. Those passing by wag their heads and say, "If you are the Son of God, come down from the cross." The chief priests and the scribes and the elders echo the mockery: "He saved others; he cannot save himself."[2]

Make no mistake: Jesus can descend from the cross and save Himself at any moment. It isn't the nails that keep Him there. What keeps Him there is what placed Him there—His passion to do the will of His Father, and His love for sinners like you and me.

Without their knowing it, the mocking words these onlookers utter do in fact reveal the uniqueness of the Savior's death and why it mattered. In their spiritual blindness they in effect express sublime spiritual truth. For Jesus cannot both save Himself and save you and me. It's precisely because He refused to save Himself that He's able to save others.

It would be necessary for Him to die even if it were for your sin alone or my sin alone. That's why you and I are fully responsible for this tragic death. As John Stott wisely observed, "Before we can begin to see the cross as something done *for* us, we have to see it as something done *by* us."[3]

Crushing Darkness

For hours we see Him hanging suspended between heaven and earth in a pain we can't imagine—and yet without complaint, without protest. Instead, we hear this: "Father, forgive them, for they know not what they do."[4]

Meanwhile, at midday, a darkness comes over the land—not from an eclipse or overcast skies, but a supernatural darkness, an atmospheric confirmation of the judgment of God. Can you imagine such a gloom? It's a darkness you can feel.

Even the sky reflects what is happening to the Son of God. Jesus is being made to drink from that cup which He had asked at Gethsemane to be removed. He is being made to experience the full fury of the wrath of God—the intense, righteous hatred of God for sin, a wrath that has been stored up beginning with Adam's sin and extending to all of your sin and mine, and to all the sin to the end of this world's history.

The sinless One—innocent and holy Himself—is made the object of that vast and vile immensity of sin. This is His severest test, His cruelest and most demanding ordeal, a torment far beyond the pain of His physical suffering.

Able to Bear It No Longer

In this strange, unnatural darkness, by the flickering light of the soldiers' torches, we step closer to the cross to watch and listen.

Suddenly His face contorts in a display of anguish more terrible than anything we've yet seen. He can restrain Himself no longer. He screams out, "My God, my God!"

Why have you forsaken me?

> Suddenly He can restrain Himself no longer.

"Nowhere in all the Bible," writes one author, "do we encounter any mystery that so staggers the mind and shocks the Christian consciousness as this tortured cry from the lips of our dying Savior."[5]

The cry is a question—but Jesus is not accusing His Father; nor is He perplexed as to why He's dying. It's a question from David's words in Psalm 22, and on the cross our Lord is fulfilling that messianic Psalm. But Jesus is also doing more than that. He's experiencing on the cross what no one in human history ever has or ever will experience. He's receiving what you and I should be receiving—His Father's full and furious wrath. He's experiencing what every other human being in history deserves and which He alone does *not* deserve.

And He's experiencing it *alone.*

True Aloneness

After my father died, I gathered with our family at a funeral home to choose the casket and arrange specifics for the memorial service. As I drove away from the funeral home, I made it only about two hundred yards before I broke down and wept, and had to pull the car over and stop.

This wasn't the first time I had cried after my father's death, but it was the first time I had cried *alone,* and the tears and the grief were so strong. Cars streamed past me, their passengers and drivers unaware of what was taking place in my car, and I vividly remember how alone I felt.

But in truth I wasn't alone, because only two hundred yards away were people who loved me with all their hearts.

To be comforted, all I needed to do was turn around and go back to the funeral home. I felt alone—but I wasn't really.

For me, personally, the sense of aloneness in that moment was overwhelming; yet I know that many others have experienced a depth of loneliness or even abandonment and rejection far worse than anything I went through. Many have wept as I did, but could never be assured there was someone nearby they could turn to for comfort, whether two hundred yards away or two hundred miles.

> There in the Father's sight is the monstrous, unbounded totality of human sin resting upon one Man.

And yet, even in comparison to such unbearable experiences, there's Someone else whose pain of isolation and abandonment goes infinitely deeper.

Before being nailed to the cross, Jesus already knew what it meant to be forsaken; He has become intimately acquainted with being rejected or abandoned by men. Yet whenever it happened, He could always say, "Though forsaken by men, I am not alone, for My Father is always with Me."

But not now.

He who for all eternity has never been alone is now wholly abandoned. Such utter desolation has never even existed before in all eternity, because of the infinite love and fellowship of the Trinity, which can never be broken. But now the incarnate Son must be forsaken by the Father...because the Father is holy, and there in the Father's sight is "the most grotesque, most obscene mass of sin in the history of the world," as R. C. Sproul termed it.[6] It's the monstrous sight of the unbounded totality of human sin resting upon one Man.

Therefore that Man must be utterly removed from the presence of the holy God, utterly separated, as far as the east is from the west.

Jesus doesn't just *feel* forsaken; He *is* forsaken. In an unfathomable mystery at that moment, as God's wrath is poured upon Him as the substitute for our sin, Jesus is rejected by God. His Father turns away from Him. It isn't a deceptive feeling; it is *reality.*

In Gethsemane, when Jesus looked into the cup, this is what He had seen. This is what had staggered Him.

The Miracle

What could possibly be more amazing? And what greater reason can there be for you and me at this very moment to praise and thank Him?

The personal desolation Christ is experiencing on the cross is what you and I should be experiencing—but instead, Jesus is bearing it, and bearing it all alone.

Why alone?

He's alone so that we might never be alone.

He cries out to God, "Why have You forsaken Me?" so that you and I will never have to make a similar cry. He was cut off from His Father so that we can boldly say, "Nothing shall separate us from the love of God in Christ Jesus."

He's forsaken so that we might be forgiven.

Please don't ever grow overfamiliar with forgiveness. What a miracle it is! What a gift from God! Our forgiveness is a fact that not only was accomplished through Christ's rejection and abandonment on the cross, but was confirmed and validated in the most incredibly glorious way possible: "Christ has indeed been raised from the dead," Paul proclaims, and it's the most thrilling and affirming part of the good news; for "if Christ has not been raised, your faith is futile; you are still in your sins."[7]

Precisely and only because of Christ's death and resurrection, there can be no more condemnation for sin for us who believe: "Who is to condemn? Christ Jesus is the one who died—more than that, who was raised—who is at the right hand of God, who indeed is interceding for us."[8] Nothing in all creation is more steeped in the miraculous than the fact of your forgiveness and mine.

In the last twenty-four hours alone, I have sinned more than enough to be justly judged by God. But instead of condemning me, He forgives me. And that forgiveness is derived only from that One suspended between heaven and earth in utter abandonment from God.

God, in abandoning His Son, is treating Jesus as a sinner so that He can treat you and me—who *are* sinners—as if we were righteous…all because of Jesus.

Thank You that the future Day of the Lord
will not be a day of wrath for me,
but a day of rejoicing—all because You drank the cup dry,
Lord Jesus…all because You suffered death
and separation from the Father as my substitute.
You drank the cup that I should have drained.
You bore the abandonment that should have been mine.
You were utterly alone so that I might never be alone.

Oh, how can I thank You enough?
You endured this suffering so that
today and tomorrow and forever
I'm alive to freely and joyfully praise You.

So in this very moment I offer You
thanksgiving and praise, Jesus, my Savior!
And I will indeed worship You forever.

Notes

1. Mathew 27:28–30
2. Matthew 27:39–42
3. John R. W. Stott, *The Cross of Christ* (Downers Grove, Illinois: InterVarsity Press, 1986), 59–60.
4. Luke 23:34
5. Richard Allen Bodey, *Voice from the Cross: Classic Sermons on the Seven Last Words of Christ* (Grand Rapids: Kregel, 2000), 57–8.
6. R. C. Sproul, 84.
7. 1 Corinthians 15:20, 17 (NIV)
8. Romans 8:34

Chapter Seven

WHAT GOD
UNDERSTANDS

*The God on whom we rely knows
what suffering is all about—not merely in the way
that God knows everything, but by experience.*
D. A. CARSON

Prior to the release of *The Passion of the Christ*, highly publicized voices expressed concern (unfounded, it turns out) whether this film would revive widespread anti-Semitic actions and accusations against the Jews as "Christ-killers." In the same month the movie opened, *Newsweek* magazine filled its front cover with a close-up of actor Jim Caviezel as the bloodied and battered Christ, plus this blaring headline: "Who Really Killed Jesus?"

That question is a valid one (although the article inside the magazine seemed primarily intended to undermine public confidence in the reliability of Scripture). It's also a question for which the Bible gives an unmistakably clear reply—though the answer still seems surprising to so many.

Who really killed Jesus?

Not my first thought.

God did.

That's who sent Him to the cross, crushing Him beneath the weight of our sins.

> Our heavenly Father knew suffering that infinitely exceeds anything we'll ever encounter.

Years ago, I was with a pastor who told me of a man in his church who one day was cleaning his gun with his son. The unthinkable happened—the gun went off, and the little boy was accidentally killed.

This pastor prayed in desperation as he sat with the distraught father, for he was at a loss to know any comfort he could bring. Then he sensed the Lord saying this to him: "Tell him I understand. Tell him I killed My son—except, it wasn't an accident."

Our heavenly Father always understands our suffering, for at Calvary, He knew suffering that infinitely exceeds anything we'll ever encounter.

Dark Hours

I'm not trying to minimize human suffering. I don't consider myself to have suffered to any great extent, and one of the most humbling experiences I have is to relate to people who are suffering in ways that are unimaginable to me, especially when they come to me for counsel. What can I say? I have so little in my own background to draw upon.

But I do know that in our time of deepest affliction, none of us find comfort by endlessly focusing on that suffering. There's an element of mystery in all our suffering, and in this life we can't fully understand it, yet we face a subtle temptation to relive and review our suffering. That's an exercise that will never bring rest and release. What *will* bring rest and release is spending more time meditating on the cross and the God of the cross.

So I point to the cross of Christ, for there's no greater encouragement, and no greater motivation for everything God has called you to do in life, than to recognize His love for you in *His* darkest hour, and to receive His care for you in *your* darkest hour.

Those dark times of temptation, trial, and hardship are inevitable for you and for me and for everyone we love. As D. A. Carson points out, all you have to do is live long enough and you'll suffer. You and I and every Christian we know will eventually suffer, if we haven't already; it's our unavoidable experience in a fallen world.

But in Gethsemane and at Calvary, we find what we need to prepare ourselves for suffering, and to sustain us in suffering.

It's a preparation that braces us for those abrupt announcements that come so unexpected:

She wants a divorce.

You're being laid off.

The test came back…you've got cancer.

Your baby—I'm sorry, he's dead.

It's a fallen world, and therefore we will all suffer. So we must prepare, because the ideal time to be educated about suffering is never in the midst of it. We need to be trained *prior to* suffering, so that we may be fully sustained *in* suffering.

Incomparable Source

However, as we look to the cross and Gethsemane for this preparation, there's a distinction we need to make: Our suffering does not truly compare to His.

Occasionally people speak of their "Gethsemane experience." But you and I never go through anything like what Jesus did at Gethsemane, and we are respectful and wise never to refer to our experiences in those terms. You and I will never be given this cup to drink.

Moreover, you and I have never

> We never go through anything like what Jesus did at Gethsemane.

been, and will never be, abandoned by God. I know sometimes it feels that He's abandoned us; I've felt that way. But those are deceptive feelings, because the One who drank this cup says to you and me, "<u>I will never leave you nor forsake you</u>." We may occasionally <u>feel alone, but we never truly are alone.</u>

And yet His suffering does become the highest and best source of comfort in our own distress. For if He endured so much more than I will ever have to, then can't He comfort me in my lesser suffering? Yes, absolutely.

So we read Hebrews 4:16 with new appreciation: "Let us then with confidence draw near to the throne of grace, that we may receive mercy and find grace to help in time of need"—in our own dark hour of suffering.

Always Enough

We notice in Scripture that at the close of Christ's agony in Gethsemane, God sent an angel to Jesus to strengthen Him. Alexander Whyte, the famous Scottish preacher of the 1800s, once said that in heaven, once he had seen Christ, he wanted his next conversation there to be with this angel. "Who knows," Whyte explained, "what depths of suffering this angel came to witness?"

But in our own depths of suffering, the Father doesn't send an angel; He sends us the *Savior*. In our ordeals, we are given comfort and strength *by Jesus Himself*.

The first physician to die of AIDS in the United Kingdom was a young Christian who had contracted the virus while doing medical research in Zimbabwe. In his final days, his powers of communication began to fail him. He struggled with increasing difficulty to express his thoughts to his wife, and on one occasion his wife simply could not understand his message.

> With a faltering hand he wrote the letter J.

The young man took a notepad and with a faltering hand wrote the letter J.

His wife ran through her mental dictionary several words beginning with J, but none was right.

Then she said to her husband, "Jesus?"

That was the right word.

Jesus was with them. That was all either of them needed to know. *Because that is always enough.*

Regardless of how dark a day becomes, regardless of the severity of the anguish we will experience, *He is always present*…and *that is sufficient.* The One at God's right hand, the One who on this earth suffered so uniquely, is the One who "always lives to make intercession" for us (Hebrews 7:25).

"We little know," Spurgeon writes, "what we owe to our Savior's prayers. When we reach the hilltops of heaven, and look back upon all the way whereby the Lord our God hath led us, how we shall praise Him who, before the eternal throne, undid the mischief which Satan was doing upon earth. How shall we thank Him because He never held His peace, but day and night pointed to the wounds upon His hands, and carried our names upon His breastplate!"[1]

Even in the glory of heaven, the wounds of the Lamb who was slain continue to bring blessing our way...especially in our own darkest hour.

Lord God, there is so much suffering in our lives.
Enable me to prepare and equip both myself and
others for the inevitable hardships we will face,
that we might glorify You in the midst of our suffering.
Enable me to do this by centering my life
on the cross of Your Son, Jesus Christ.
By the power of Your Holy Spirit,
help me continue to watch and pray.

Thank You for the comfort that is ours in the cross.
Thank You, God, that You will wipe away
every tear in the eyes of Your servants,
because of the sacrifice of the Lamb of God.

Lord Jesus, I glory in Your cross!

Notes

1. Charles H. Spurgeon, *Morning and Evening,* January 11, evening meditation.

Chapter Eight

ASSURANCE
AND JOY

Nothing in my hand I bring;
Simply to your cross I cling.
Augustus Toplady

It was a Monday morning, and as I stepped toward my office, I saw Melody, one of the secretaries. Melody is a joy and a gem—energy and enthusiasm personified. There's never anything calm about what she's saying.

Melody also has cancer—and she's bald from chemotherapy treatments.

On that Monday morning, Melody greeted me with even more enthusiasm than normal. "Oh, C. J.," she was saying, "Yesterday, yesterday…"

The day before was the long-anticipated Sunday where our church took up a special offering in support of our mission fund. In preparation for it, we had gone through a month-long time of teaching about our church's missions, as well as instruction about giving. The members of Covenant Life Church in Gaithersburg, Maryland—where I've served for twenty-seven years—are remarkable in how they've always given heroically and joyfully, and now we were asking them to sacrificially give even more.

When that Sunday came for the special offering, the mood throughout the congregation was one of thrilling excitement. In the lobby where I greet people, I was almost mobbed by those who wanted to express their support and anticipation for this privilege of giving. They were so glad this day had come (and their excitement made me wonder how many pastors ever have such an experience).

Now on this Monday morning, Melody was still glowing from how we all had experienced God's grace. She was getting tears in her eyes. "What a great Sunday in the history of this church," she told me. "Thank you for giving us this opportunity to give!"

I stood there feeling so humbled, feeling I was on holy ground. Melody has spent many days lying sick in bed and looking death in the eye. But there's a joy in her heart and a power from God upon her that I can only behold and envy and rejoice in.

What explains that joy, that power?

Melody has contemplated what happened at Gethsemane. So when you talk with her about suffering, it's the Savior's suffering on her behalf that she's more aware of than any adversity she's experienced. Melody's also aware that because of the Savior's unique suffering for her on the cross, she is deriving indescribable comfort from Him. And what she finds is a new song in her heart that is ultimately for God's praise and His glory.

It's the gospel that sustains Melody with personal assurance of God's grace and love. She has discovered something that the prophet Habakkuk came to know. When life did not make sense to Habakkuk, when all he saw on the horizon was appalling and dreadful suffering for himself and God's people, he responded this way: "Yet I will rejoice in the LORD; I will take joy in the God of my salvation."[1] He turned his attention away from suffering and fixed it upon the more serious and critical issue of salvation.

In your own times of severe distress, which are you more aware of—your suffering or your salvation? What the Puritan Thomas Watson recognized will always be true for us: "Your sufferings are not so great as your sins: Put these two in the balance, and see which weighs heaviest."[2] We can rejoice even amid affliction when we recognize the seriousness of our sins and their just penalty, and the forgiveness and salvation we're so graciously granted through Christ's death.

Personal Assurance of His Love

As a pastor, few things affect me more than interacting with those who, unlike Melody, are unaware of God's personal love for *them*. Normally there isn't a week that goes by where I'm not talking with someone who hasn't understood this truth—"Christ loved *me* and gave Himself for *me*"—in personal experience.

> Christ loved me... Christ gave Himself for me.

Those words are the apostle Paul's: "I have been crucified with Christ," he wrote. "It is no longer I who live, but Christ who lives in me. And the life I now live in the flesh I live by faith in the Son of God, who loved me and gave himself for me."[3] In his commentary on that verse, Leon Morris says this statement "is for me personally the most moving text in the whole of Scripture."

Australian theologian Peter Jensen notes Paul's significant use in this verse of the past tense— not that "Christ loves me," as we might expect him to say, but that "Christ *loved* me." Paul "could not graduate beyond the Cross of Jesus as the source and power of his religion, as the place at which he gained assurance, as the demonstration beyond any other need of proof of the grace and love of God."[4]

Every Christian has the same privilege of saying those words about the cross and knowing this truth personally:

"The Son of God loved *me*…the Son of God gave Himself for *me*." That's why my heart aches to be with any believer who lacks the certainty of God's specific, passionate, and personal love.

Sinclair Ferguson says we lack this assurance of His personal grace to us "because we fail to focus on that spot where He has revealed it."[5] And "that spot" is obviously the cross.

The distractions that turn us away from the cross are so incessant and so numerous. But failing to focus on the right spot has serious consequences. So here's my question for you: In the last week, what was your primary preoccupation in your life? What was your spiritual focus? Was it on that spot where God most reveals His personal love for you—the cross? Or was it on your own circumstances, your own condition, your own concerns? Was your preoccupation with your personal pursuit of godliness? Growth in godliness must be pursued, but never apart from joyful gratitude for the cross.

That's why in my own spiritual diet—and I recommend this for yours as well—a consistent ingredient is the study of the cross, primarily from Scripture but also from many of the outstanding books that have been written about the cross from a strong biblical perspective.[6] Let there never be a lengthy period of time where you aren't receiving inspiration and instruction related directly to the cross, since that's where we find a fresh, sustaining conviction of His personal love.

Martin Luther once wrote that he taught the gospel "again and again, because I greatly fear that after we have laid our head to rest, it will soon be forgotten and will again disappear." That's my great fear as well—that after hearing about the cross, we'll lay down our heads to rest and quietly forget it, instead of dwelling upon it and deriving the continual strength and assurance we need.

> Will we lay down our heads to rest and quietly forget the cross?

We have a constant tendency to stop remembering the cross, and to start depending on legalism and self-effort. The danger is relentless. So I urge you every day to "preach the gospel to yourself," as Jerry Bridges calls it in his book *The Discipline of Grace*. Doing so, he says, means "you continually face up to your own sinfulness and then flee to Jesus through faith in His shed blood and righteous life."[7]

By preaching to ourselves the gospel, we easily accept Spurgeon's pithy observation: "Jesus is 'mighty to save,' the best proof of which lies in the fact that He has saved you."[8]

Cultivating Joy

And the inevitable result of preaching the gospel to yourself will be a pronounced joy, an infectious joy, a consistent joy.

Like nothing else, the gospel creates joy; it's both the

I don't exude infectious joy.

source and the object of our joy. The gospel alone allows us to obey the biblical directive to "serve the LORD with gladness."[9] Joy is a command. You may be working hard and serving the Lord faithfully, but if you aren't serving with gladness, you aren't serving Him appropriately or representing Him accurately.[10]

Are you someone who's consistently joyful and continually aware that the joy of the Lord is your strength?[11] Or do you normally appear to others to be someone who's burdened, busy, and easily bothered?

When the disciples returned to Jesus after a successful ministry trip and reported excitedly, "Lord, even the demons are subject to us in your name!" Jesus responded, "Do not rejoice in this, that the spirits are subject to you, but rejoice that your names are written in heaven."[12] He wasn't trying to minimize the joy one derives from ministry success. But He was drawing their attention away from that to *primary* joy—a joy that takes precedence over the experience of spiritual power. And that is the joy that comes from the gospel, the gospel that writes our names in heaven.

If you're centering your life on the gospel and the cross—if you're abiding hard by the cross, as Spurgeon says, and searching the mystery of Christ's wounds—then you will be captured by joy. And in these days or years you have left on earth, what could be better?

So cultivate this joy…by continually meditating on the

gospel. Let the cross always be the treasure of your heart, your best and highest thought…and your passionate pre-occupation.

"Nothing in my hand I bring, simply to Your cross I cling."
Lord, I bring nothing to You.
I do not bring to You my own righteousness.
What a joke that would be!
How repulsive even the thought of that must be to You.

No, nothing, nothing in my hands do I bring,
except my sin in need of forgiveness.
I come to You in spiritual poverty and helplessness,
looking to You for the grace that flows
from the fountain filled with Your holy blood.

Simply to Your cross I cling.
O Lord Jesus Christ, I wrap my arms
and the entirety of my heart around Your cross!

Thank You, Jesus, that You loved me!
Thank You that You gave Yourself for me!
I rejoice in Your love and acceptance of me.

Notes

1. Habakkuk 3:18
2. Thomas Watson, *The Art of Divine Contentment.*
3. Galatians 2:20
4. Peter Jensen, "The Cross & Faith: The Good News of God's Wrath," *Christianity Today,* March 2004, 45.
5. Sinclair Ferguson, *Grow in Grace* (Carlisle, Pennsylvania: Banner of Truth, 1989), 59.
6. I recommend *The Gospel for Real Life* and *The Discipline of Grace* by Jerry Bridges; *The Cross of Christ* by John Stott; *Saved from What?* by R. C. Sproul; *The Passion of Jesus Christ* by John Piper; and *The Message of Salvation* by Philip Ryken.
7. Jerry Bridges, *The Discipline of Grace* (Colorado Springs: NavPress, 1994), 58.
8. Charles H. Spurgeon, *Morning and Evening,* January 14, evening meditation.
9. Psalm 100:2
10. see Deuteronomy 28:47
11. Philippians 4:4; Nehemiah 8:10
12. Luke 10:17–20

What Are You Centered On?

Sometimes the most important truths are the easiest to forget. It's time to get back to the starting point of the Christian life—the cross of Christ. Tap into the gospel's power and see how a cross centered focus can transform your life today!

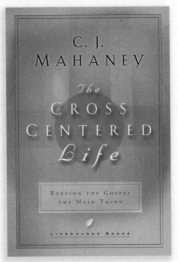

"Every Timothy needs a Paul. C.J. Mahaney is mine...and this book contains his life-message. Read it yourself, and let God realign your life."

—Joshua Harris, pastor and bestselling author